GET  MAKOTO+

EVERY MONTH AUTOMATICALLY
(and at a discount)

https://www.MakotoPlus.com

You'll get:

Download the Latest Makoto Issue | Read 3 Full Back Issues Online | Reusable TheJapanShop.com Coupon | Monthly Freebies

誠 MAKOTO

e-zine for learners of Japanese

THEJAPANSHOP.COM
VOLUME 5 | ISSUE 50 | April 2022

ご 購入
（こうにゅう）
ありがとう
ございます。

Thank you so much
for your purchase!

Four years ago this month, Yumi and I held our breath and launched the first Makoto issue.

It was terrifying.

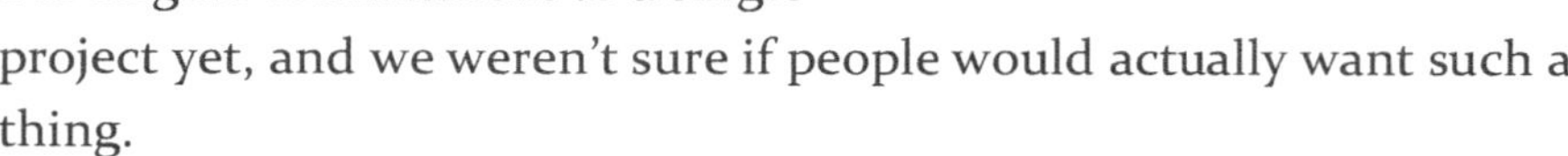

We had, of course, published quite a few books by that time, but a monthly digital magazine? It would be our largest commitment to a single project yet, and we weren't sure if people would actually want such a thing.

But I remembered my time as a beginner in the late 1990s. Mangajin was my favorite resource for learning Japanese, and I knew there had to be a demand for something like that. Of course, we didn't have the resources to include actual manga, but what I liked best about Mangajin was the sentence breakdowns, and that was something we could do. Mangajin also made sure to include tons of notes on Japanese culture. Culture and language (especially Japanese) cannot be separated.

Well, we still don't have manga in our Makoto magazine, but we continue to follow Mangajin's lead in other areas.

For four years and fifty issues—ありがとうございます! Yumi and I are grateful for your patronage. We hope Makoto will continue to be a useful tool to help grow your Japanese ability.

Clay & Yumi

WHO ARE WE?

Nearly two decades ago, Clay & Yumi began **TheJapanesePage.com**, one of the Internet's oldest and largest *free* Japanese instructional sites with hundreds of free articles for beginners of Japanese.

They also maintain **TheJapanShop.com**, a web-store specializing in materials to help learners of Japanese.

Have any questions or comments? Contact us at **help@thejapanshop.com**

In this Issue:

LAUGHS, JOKES, RIDDLES, AND PUNS

Scan for Recording

鯉がいる池のそばに、看板があった。そこには、こう書いてあった。「鯉の餌10円」これを読んだ友だちは、10円玉を池に投げ込んだ。

（解説）看板に書いてあったのは、「鯉の餌は10円で売っています」という意味だったが、友だちは「10円玉」が鯉の餌になると勘違いした。でも、鯉は、10円玉は食べられない。

There was a signboard near a pond with carp. It said there, "Carp food 10 yen". When my friend read this, he threw a 10 yen coin into the pond.

（Explanation）What was written on the signboard meant that "Carp food is sold for 10 yen", but my friend misunderstood that the "10 yen coin" would be used as food for the carp. However, carp can't eat a ten-yen coin.

Vocabulary:

ジョーク *jo-ku*—a joke

鯉 *koi*—koi; carp

（が）いる *(ga) iru*—there is/are (living things) [Noun + （が）いる]

Vocabulary Continued

池のそばに *ike no soba ni*—near a pond [池 (pond) + の (modifier; is used to tell the location) + そば (near; close; beside; vicinity) + に (expresses the location of existence)]

看板があった *kanban ga atta*—there was a signboard [看板 (signboard; sign) + が (identifies what performs the action; emphasizes the preceding word) + あった (there was/were; plain past form of ある (to have; to be; there is/are))]

そこには *soko ni wa*—there [そこ (there) + には (に (expresses the location of existence) + は (adds emphasis); puts more emphasis and restriction on the preceding word)]

こう書いてあった *kou kaite atta*—the (signboard) said; said: [こう (refers to the speaker's location or idea) + 書いてあった (from 書く (to write; to compose); ~てあった is the plain past form of ~てある (is used when the result of an intentional action still affects the current state or the result exists until the moment when the speaker describes it); how to form: Verb て-form + あった)]

「鯉の餌10円」 *「koi no esa juu en」*—"Carp food 10 yen" [「」 (quotation marks; " ") + 鯉 (koi; carp) + の (of; 's; modifier) + 餌 ((animal) feed; pet food; bait) + 10円 (ten yen; 円 is the Japanese monetary unit)]

これを読んだ友だちは *kore o yonda tomodachi wa*—as for the friend who read this [これ (this; this one) + を (indicates the direct object of action) + 読んだ (read; plain past form of 読む (to read)) + 友だち (friend; companion) + は (indicates the sentence topic)]

10円玉を池に投げ込んだ *juu en dama o ike ni nagekonda*—(he) threw a 10 yen coin into the pond [10円玉 (10 yen coin; 円 (yen) + 玉 (coin; sphere)) + を (indicates the direct object of action) + 池 (pond) + に (into; expresses the direction) + 投げ込んだ (plain past form of 投げ込む

Vocabulary Continued

(to throw; to cast))]

解説 *kaisetsu*—explanation; commentary

看板に書いてあったのは *kanban ni kaite atta no wa*—what was written on the signboard [看板 (signboard; sign) + に (on; expresses the location of existence) + 書いてあった (from 書く (to write; to compose); ~てあった is the plain past form of ~てある (is used when the result of an intentional action still affects the current state or the result exists until the moment when the speaker describes it)) + の (a nominalizer that acts like a noun; placeholder for nouns) + は (indicates the sentence topic)]

「鯉の餌は10円で売っています」 *「koi no esa wa juu en de utte imasu」*—"Carp food is sold for 10 yen" [「」(quotation marks; " ") + 鯉 (koi; carp) + の (of; modifier) + 餌 ((animal) feed; pet food) + は (indicates the sentence topic) + 10円 (10 yen) + で (for; indicates a total amount of something (money, time, etc.)) + 売っています (is sold; ています-form of 売る (to sell) which is used to describe a continuous action; how to form: Verb て-form + います)]

「鯉の餌は10円で売っています」という意味だった *「koi no esa wa juu en de utte imasu」 to iu imi datta*—meant that "Carp food is sold for 10 yen" [「鯉の餌は10円で売っています」("Carp food is sold for 10 yen") + という (that; called; that says) + 意味 (meaning; sense; significance) + だった (plain form past tense marker which is typically used with nouns and な-adjectives)]

が *ga*—but; however

友だちは *tomodachi wa*—a friend [友だち (friend; companion) + は (indicates the sentence topic)]

Vocabulary Continued

「10円玉」が鯉の餌になる *「juu en dama」 ga koi no esa ni naru*—the "10 yen coin" becomes the food for the carp [**「10円玉」** ("10 yen coin") + **が** (identifies what performs the action) + **鯉** (koi; carp) + **の** (of; for; modifier) + **餌** ((animal) feed; pet food) + **に** (expresses the result of change) + **なる** (to become; to turn; to end up)]

と勘違いした *to kanchigai shita*—misunderstood that [**と** (used for quoting (thoughts, speech, etc.)) + **勘違いした** (misunderstood; plain past form of **勘違いする** (confuse oneself; get something wrong; get the wrong idea))]

でも *demo*—however; but

10円玉は食べられない *juu en dama wa taberarenai*—(carp) can't eat a ten-yen coin [**10円玉** (ten-yen coin) + **は** (is used with the potential form of a verb) + **食べられない** (can't eat; plain potential negative form of **食べる** (to eat))]

VOCABULARY

Learn Useful Words, Phrases, and Sayings

Scan for Recording

<ruby>身<rt>み</rt></ruby>を<ruby>固<rt>かた</rt></ruby>める

mi o katameru

settle down; get married and raise a family; tie the knot

ⓘ This can be a synonym for marriage. Use only with men.

> The original meaning may have been to armor oneself, which evolved into putting one's attire in order.

EXAMPLE SENTENCE:

Example Sentence

おい、<ruby>君<rt>きみ</rt></ruby>、そろそろ<ruby>身<rt>み</rt></ruby>を<ruby>固<rt>かた</rt></ruby>めたらどうだ?

oi, kimi, sorosoro mi o katametara dou da?

Hey, shouldn't you start thinking about settling down? (Casual male speech)

VOCABULARY:

おい *oi*—Hey! (only to be used by males among peers or by superiors to subordinates, otherwise it can be a little rude; male speech)

君 *kimi*—you

そろそろ *sorosoro*—soon; to be about time for...

7

VOCABULARY

Learn Useful Words, Phrases, and Sayings

Vocabulary Continued

身 *mi*—body [doesn't really mean "body", more like "one's life" or "lifestyle"]

を *o*—(direct object marker)

固め *katame*—*masu*-stem of 固める (to harden)

~たら ~*tara*—if~; when~; after~ [used for supposition;

Construction:

Step 1. Conjugate verb to past tense: 固める→固めた

Step 2. Add ら after it: 固めた→固めたら

(Even though たら is a particle and isn't actually in the past tense, this may help you remember it.)]

どうだ *dou da*—how about~?; why not~? why don't you ~? [sounds very male-ish speech and casual; どうですか？ is more polite; ～たらどう？ is very casual used among close friends; (どう (how) + だ (copula)); it has no question marker か, but we know it is a question by the flow of the conversation; the speaker is talking to his peer or to a younger person]

身を固めたらどうだ *mi o katametara dou da*—how about settling down? [literally, "why don't you solidify yourself?" This is only used toward men.]

~たらどうだ？ (very male), ~たらどう？ (very casual), ~たらどうですか？ (polite)—why don't you~? how about~? [used to encourage or advise someone to do something]

しずおか
Shizuoka 静岡

Japanese: 静岡県 *shizuoka ken*
Capital: 静岡 *shizuoka*
Population: 3,637,998 (December 1, 2019)

DID YOU KNOW?

Shizuoka was the area Tokugawa Ieyasu controlled until he conquered much of the Kanto region (present day Tokyo and surrounding area). Mt. Fuji shares a border with Shizuoka and Yamanashi prefectures.

PLACES TO SEE:

- **Mt. Fuji**—officially open for climbing during July and August. The volcano is free from snow and transportation and support huts are open to the public during those months.

- **Izu Peninsula**—a resort area full of hot springs, beaches, and a clear view of Mt. Fuji.

- **Sumpu Castle**—the retirement home of Tokugawa Ieyasu. Built in 1585, it was dismantled during the Meiji Restoration. Today, the area is mostly park grounds, but the castle is being reconstructed.

- **Fuji Speedway**—an international race track where the Japanese F1 is held.

- **Atami Castle**—a 1959 concrete reconstruction, Atami Castle has a spectacular view of the city of Atami and about 200 cherry blossom trees.

FAMOUS FOR:

- **Mt. Fuji**—straddling the borders of Shizuoka and Yamanashi prefectures, Fuji-san is the most iconic image of Japan. It is a volcano and talk of it erupting soon is often heard. The last major eruption was in 1707. It stands 3,776.24 meters (12,389 feet).

- **Tea**—Shizuoka accounts for 45% of Japan's overall tea production.

- Home to **Honda Motor Company**, **Kawai Pianos**, **Yamaha**, **Sony**, and **Suzuki Motor Company**.

- **Tokugawa Ieyasu** retired in Shizuoka and was originally buried at Kunōzan Tōshō-gū (later moved to Nikko in Tochigi prefecture).

耳を傾ける
Mimi o Katamukeru (Bend One's Ear)

Scan for Recording

「耳を傾ける」の意味は、相手の話を一生懸命に聞くとか、集中して聞くという意味です。この言葉の語源は、動作から来ています。相手の話を一生懸命に聞こうとするとき、体を前に乗り出したり、耳の向きを変えたりします。ここから「耳を傾ける」という言葉ができました。友だちや先生、親などからアドバイスを受けるときは、耳を傾けましょう。

"*Mimi o Katamukeru*" means to listen actively to what the other person is saying, or to listen in a concentrated manner. The etymology of this word comes from an "action". When we listen intently to what the other person has to say, we lean forward or turn our ears. This is where the word "*Mimi o Katamukeru*" came from. Let's listen very closely when receiving advice from friends, teachers, parents, etc.

Vocabulary

語源 etymology; origin of a word

耳を傾ける to bend one's ear; to give an ear to; to listen carefully; to lend an ear [耳 (ear) + を (indicates the direct object of action) + 傾ける (to bend; to incline; to lean; to tilt)]

「耳を傾ける」の意味は *"mimi o katamukeru"* means; the meaning of *"mimi o katamukeru"* [「耳を傾ける」(*"mimi o katamukeru* (bend one's ear)") + の (of; modifier) + 意味 (meaning; significance; sense) + は (indicates the sentence topic)]

相手の話を一生懸命に聞く to listen actively to what the other person is saying [相手 (other person; partner; companion) + の (of; modifier) + 話 (conversation; talk; speech) + を (indicates the direct object of action) + 一生懸命に (actively; with great enthusiasm; with all one's strength; heartily; intently; に is added to 一生懸命 (as hard as one can; with utmost effort) to turn it into an adverbial form) + 聞く (to listen; to hear)]

とか and/or [connecting particle which is used to list the same kind of multiple things and imply there are other items that could be included in the list]

集中して聞く to listen in a concentrated manner [集中して (て-form of 集中する (to concentrate; to focus) which is used to modify the next verb 聞く) + 聞く (to listen; to hear)]

という意味 such a meaning [という (is used to define, describe, and generally just talk about the thing itself) + 意味 (sense; meaning)]

です be; is

この言葉の語源は the etymology of this word [この (this) + 言葉 (word; term; expression) + の (of; modifier) + 語源 (etymology; derivation of a word; origin of word) + は (indicates the sentence topic)]

動作から from action [動作 (action; movement (of the body); motion) + から (from)]

来ています come; is/are coming; has come [ています-form of 来る (to come) which is used to describe a continuous action; how to form: Verb て-form + います]

相手の話を一生懸命に聞こうとする try to listen intently to what the other person has to say [相手 (other person; companion) + の (of; modifier) + 話 (talk; conversation) + を (indicates the direct object of action) + 一生懸命に (actively; with great enthusiasm; intently) + 聞こうとする (try to listen; 聞こう is the plain volitional form of 聞く (to listen; to hear); 「Verb (volitional form) + とする」 means "to try to do ~; to be about to do")]

とき when; at this time [how to form: Verb (casual form) + とき]

Vocabulary Continued

体を前に乗り出したり耳の向きを変えたりします (we) lean forward or turn (our) ears [体 (body) + を (indicates the direct object of action) + 前に (forward; 前 (forward; in front) + に (expresses the direction)) + 乗り出したり (from 乗り出す (to lean forward; to set out); ~たり is used when we give examples) + 耳 (ear) + の (of; modifier) + 向き (direction; orientation) + を (indicates the direct object of action) + 変えたりします (from 変える (to change; to alter); ~たりします is the polite/ます form of ~たりする (parallel marker for verbs and adjectives)); 「~たり~たりする」 is used to list multiple actions but imply that there remains something unsaid; how to form: Verb (た-form) + り and the last verb has to be with する (plain) or します (polite)]

ここから from here [ここ (here; this point) + から (from)]

「耳を傾ける」という言葉 the word *"mimi o katamukeru"* [「耳を傾ける」 (*"mimi o katamukeru* (bend one's ear)")) + という (called; is used to define, describe, and generally just talk about the thing itself) + 言葉 (word; term; phrase)]

ができました could; was able [が (is used with the potential form of a verb) + できました (polite past form of できる (potential form of する (to do; to cause to become)))]

友だち friend; companion

や and; or; connecting particle [is used to list multiple things and imply there are other that could be included in the list; how to form: Noun + や + Noun]

先生 teacher; instructor; master; title or form of address for a doctor, lawyer, etc.

親 parent; parents; mother and father

など et cetera; etc.; and the like; and so forth

から from

アドバイスを受けるときは when receiving advice [アドバイス (advice) + を (indicates the direct object of action) + 受ける (to receive; to get) + とき (when; at this time; how to form: Verb (casual form) + とき) + は (indicates the sentence topic; adds emphasis)]

耳を傾けましょう let's listen very closely [plain volitional form of 耳を傾ける (listen very closely; bend one's ear) which is used when making a suggestion to one or more people including oneself ("let's" / "shall we")]

ANIME / MANGA PHRASE

Surprise your Japanese friends with these phrases

Please see the sound files for the pronunciation

「やっぱりたい焼きは焼き立てが一番だよね。」

アニメ「かのん」月宮あゆのセリフ

Scan for Recording

「yappari taiyaki wa yakitate ga ichiban da yo ne.」

anime 「kanon」 tsukimiya ayu no serifu

"After all, *Taiyaki* (fish-shaped pancake filled with bean jam) is best when it's freshly baked."
Line from Tsukimiya Ayu of anime "Kanon"

VOCABULARY

「」 —(quotation marks; " ")

やっぱり *yappari*—after all (is said and done); as one would expect; just as one thought

たい焼き *taiyaki*—taiyaki; fish-shaped pancake filled with bean jam [is a Japanese fish-shaped cake and its most common filling is red bean paste that is made from sweetened azuki beans]

は *wa*—(indicates the sentence topic)

焼き立て *yakitate*—freshly baked; fresh made; freshly roasted

ANIME / MANGA PHRASE

Surprise your Japanese friends with these phrases

Vocabulary Continued

が *ga*—(emphasizes the preceding word 焼き立て (freshly baked))

一番 *ichiban*—best; most

だ *da*—be; is [casual form of the polite copula です (be; is)]

よね *yo ne*—(sentence ender) [add ね when you are less sure about opinions, information, or knowledge]

アニメ「かのん」 *anime 「kanon」*—anime "Kanon" [アニメ (anime; animation; animated film) + 「」 (quotation marks; " ") + かのん (Kanon; Japanese anime)]

月宮あゆのセリフ *tsukimiya ayu no serifu*—Line from Tsukimiya Ayu [月宮あゆ (Tsukimiya Ayu) + の (of; 's; from; modifier) + セリフ (one's lines; speech; words)]

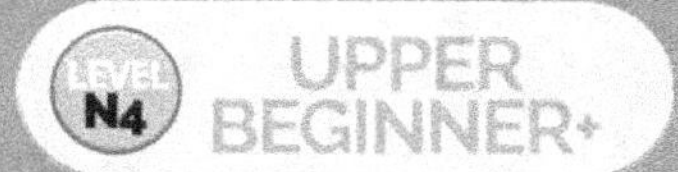

Masaoka Shiki 正岡子規
まさおかしき

今年また　花散る
ことし　　　はなち

四月十二日
しがつじゅうににち

Haiku Audio

kotoshi mata / hana chiru / shigatsu juu ni nichi
This year again | blossoms fall | on April 12

Explanation:

Explanation

（意味）今年もまた 桜 は散って
いみ　ことし　　　さくら　ち
しまいました。今日は4月１２日
　　　　　　　　　きょう　　しがつじゅうににち
です。

(Meaning) The cherry blossoms have fallen again this year too. Today is April 12.

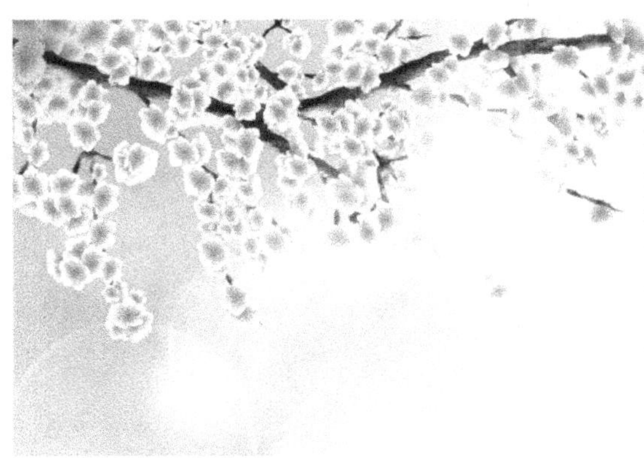

Continued

Vocabulary

今年 this year [今 (now; currently; present) + 年 (year)]

また also; too; as well; again

花 flower; blossom; bloom; petal

散る to fall (e.g. blossoms, leaves)

四月十二日 April 12; 12th day of April; 12th of April [四月 (April; 四 (four) + 月 (month)) + 十二日 (12th day of the month; 十二 (twelve) + 日 (day (of the month); counter for days))]

意味 meaning; significance; sense

今年もまた again this year too [今年 (this year) + も (too; also; as well) + また (again; also)]

桜は cherry blossoms [桜 (cherry tree; cherry blossom) + は (indicates the sentence topic)]

散ってしまいました has/have fallen [from 散る (to fall (e.g. blossoms, leaves)); ～てしまいました is the polite past form of ～てしまう (refers to a regrettable event or negative meaning); how to form: Verb て-form + しまいました]

今日は today [今日 (today; this day) + は (indicates the sentence topic)]

4月12日 April 12

です be; is

正岡子規 Masaoka Shiki (1867-1902) [was a Japanese poet, author, and literary critic in Meiji period. He emphasized creativity within the individual and ultimately established haiku poetry as modern literature.]

16

LEVEL **BEGINNER** JLPT N5

JLPT N5 Kanji

女

On: ジョ

Kun: おんな

Meaning: woman; female

Hint: Think of a woman dancing.

Audio of Readings

A female ninja is called *kunoichi*. If you combine hiragana *ku* く, katakana *no* ノ, and the kanji *ichi* 一 you get 女. This is also the order of the strokes: くノ一

Stroke Order:

女 く 女 女

Examples:

かのじょ
彼女 1) her; 2) girlfriend

おんな こ
女 の子 a girl

じょゆう
女優 an actress

Audio of Examples

かれ　　おんな
彼は 女 をナンパばかりする。

kare wa onna o nanpa bakari suru.

He is always hitting on women.

[*nanpa* means "to hit on" the opposite sex.]

Audio of Example

VOCABULARY:

彼 *kare*—he; him

は *wa*—(indicates the sentence topic)

LEVEL **BEGINNER**
JLPT N5

JLPT N5 Kanji

On: ジョ

Kun: おんな

Meaning: woman; female

Hint: Think of a woman dancing.

Audio of Readings

Vocabulary Continued

女 *onna*—female; woman; female sex

を *o*—(indicates the direct object of action)

ナンパ *nanpa*—hitting on women; smooth talker

ばかり *bakari*—only ~; just ~; nothing but [it is often used to express surprise, shock, and even judgement (in a negative way); how to form: Noun + ばかり]

する *suru*—to do

など

ABOUT:

When giving a non-exhaustive list, use など as you would use "etc" in English. "et cetera" "and the like" "and so forth."

HOW TO USE:

■ Add after the last entry of a non-exhaustive list.

EXAMPLES:

日本、中国、韓国**など**は、アジアの国です。

Japan, China, Korea, <u>**among others**</u> are Asian countries.

新幹線の名前は、のぞみ、ひかり、こだま**など**。

The names for Shinkansen bullet trains <u>**include**</u> Nozomi, Hikari, Kodama, <u>**etc**</u>.

Example 1

Example 2

VOCABULARY:

日本 *nihon*—Japan

中国 *chuugoku*—China

Vocabulary Continued

韓国 *kankoku*—South Korea; Republic of Korea

など *nado*—among others; etc.; and so on; and the like

は *wa*—(indicates the sentence topic)

アジアの国 *ajia no kuni*—Asian countries [アジア （Asia） ＋ の （of; modifier） ＋ 国 (country; countries; state)]

です *desu*—be; is

新幹線の名前 *shinkansen no namae*—name of bullet train; name for Shinkansen [新幹線 (bullet train; Shinkansen) ＋ の (of; for; modifier) ＋ 名前 (name)]

のぞみ *nozomi*—Nozomi [fastest Tōkaidō and Sanyō-line Shinkansen train service (stopping only at largest stations)]

ひかり *hikari*—Hikari [high-speed Tōkaidō and Sanyō-line Shinkansen train service (faster than Kodama; slower than Nozomi)]

こだま *kodama*—Kodama [slowest Tōkaidō and Sanyō-line Shinkansen train service (stopping at all stations)]

よんでみよう！LET'S READ!

Learn through reading for (very) beginners of Japanese

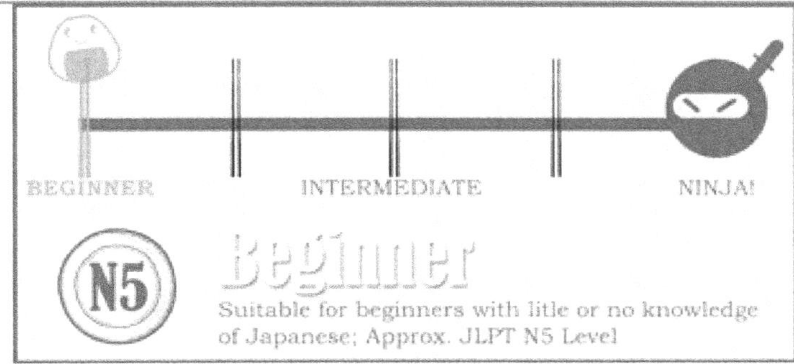

Have you only recently learned hiragana but need practice? Or perhaps, your hiragana is no problem, but you want to build your reading comprehension?

This segment is here to the rescue!

Read real Japanese—beginner level but not boring Japanese! Enjoy reading flash fiction, super short essays, and funny stories of common mistakes made by foreigners in Japan.

Best of all, the only requirement is that you can read hiragana. Vocabulary and grammar will be defined and explained.

The format is a little different from our other more advanced readers. The idea is for the reader to read the entire story three times. Each page will have a sentence or two in hiragana (with spaces between words for you to see "words" instead of syllables) at the top and that same content in full Japanese (with furigana) at the bottom. The middle will have the glossary and grammatical explanations. Lastly, the story will be presented in Japanese without furigana. See if you can read it after going through the explanations.

If you have just learned hiragana, you may want to listen to the sound file while reading the hiragana section to practice correct pronunciation. If you have studied Japanese a bit longer, you may want to start with the bottom version and take note of the glossary for understanding.

Makoto+ members can access this in a more interactive format. To learn more:

http://MakotoPlus.com

And now...

Let's learn about...

JAPANESE STREET FOOD

PART 2: "TAIYAKI"

Normal Speed

Slow Speed

The top and bottom Japanese texts are identical in meaning. The top version is only in hiragana and includes spaces between words. The bottom version has no spaces and uses kanji with furigana. Unless you are just practicing hiragana recognition, try to work through both versions. Scan the QR codes for the sound files.

日本のストリートフード

その2　「たい焼き」

JAPANESE STREET FOOD, PART 2: "TAIYAKI"

たい　と　いう　さかな　の　かたち　を　した　おかし　で、なか
に　あんこ　が　たっぷり　はいって　います。

GLOSSARY AND NOTES

日本のストリートフード *nihon no sutori-to fu-do*—street food in Japan; street food of Japan; Japanese street food [日本 (Japan) + の (of; in; 's; modifier) + ストリートフード (street food)]

その2　*sono ni*—Part 2
「たい焼き」　/*taiyaki*/ —"taiyaki" [a Japanese fish-shaped cake filled with red bean paste]

鯛という魚 *tai to iu sakana*—a fish called *tai* [鯛 (*tai*; sea bream; species of reddish-brown Pacific sea bream) + という (that; called; is used to define, describe, and generally just talk about the thing itself) + 魚 (fish)]

鯛という魚の形をしたお菓子で *tai to iu sakana no katachi o shita okashi de*—a pancake that is shaped like a fish called *tai* (sea bream) and [鯛という魚 (a fish called *tai*) + の (modifier) + 形 (form; shape; figure) + を (indicates the direct object of action) + した (plain past form of する (to do)) + お菓子 (sweet treat; cake; confectionery) + で (て-form of です (be; is) which is used to connect the next phrase, creating the meaning of "and")]

中に *naka ni*—inside [中 (inside; interior; in) + に (expresses the location of existence)]

あんこがたっぷり入っています *anko ga tappuri haitte imasu*—is well-filled with *anko* (red bean jam); be loaded with *anko* [あんこ (*anko*; red bean paste; red bean jam) + が (identifies what performs the action; emphasizes the preceding word) + たっぷり (full; in plenty; ample) + 入っています (is filled; is contained; ています-form of 入る (to contain; to go into) which is used to describe the actual condition or appearance of the subject; how to form: Verb て-form + います)]

鯛という魚の形をしたお菓子で、中にあんこがたっぷり

入っています

めいじ　じだい　から　たべられて　います。あんこ　の　かわり
に、くりーむ、ちょこれーと、きゃらめる　など　が　はいって　いる
こと　も　あります。

GLOSSARY AND NOTES

明治時代から　*meiji jidai kara*—since the Meiji era (1868 - 1912) [明治　(Meiji (1868-1912)) + 時代 (period; era) + から　(from (e.g. time, place, numerical quantity); since)]

食べられています　*taberarete imasu*—has/have been eaten; is/are eaten [ています-form of 食べられる　(plain passive positive form of 食べる　(to eat)) which is used to describe a continuous action]

あんこのかわりに　*anko no kawari ni*—instead of *anko* [あんこ　(*anko*; red bean paste; red bean jam) + の　(of; modifier) + かわりに　(instead of; in place of; as a substitute for)]

クリーム　*kuri-mu*—cream

チョコレート　*chokore-to*—chocolate

キャラメル　*kyarameru*—caramel (soft candy)

など　*nado*—et cetera; etc.; and the like; and so forth

が入っていることもあります　*ga haitte iru koto mo arimasu*—is sometimes filled (with cream, chocolate, etc.) [が　(identifies what performs the action) + 入っている　(is filled; ている-form of 入る　(to contain; to go into) which is used to describe the actual condition or appearance of the subject) + こともあります　(ます/polite form of こともある　(sometimes do); how to form: Verb (dictionary form) + こともあります)]

明治時代から食べられています。あんこのかわりに、クリーム、

チョコレート、キャラメルなどが入っていることもあります。

あにめ 「かのん」 で、 つきみや あゆ が たいやき を たべて い
た こと で、 かいがい でも ゆうめい に なりました。

GLOSSARY AND NOTES

アニメ 「かのん」 で *anime 「kanon」 de*—in the anime "Kanon" [アニメ (anime; animated cartoon; animated film; animation) + 「かのん」 ("Kanon"; 「」 (quotation marks; " ") + かのん (Kanon)) + で (in; indicates the location of action)]

月宮あゆが *tsukimiya ayu ga*—Tsukimiya Ayu [月宮あゆ (Tsukimiya Ayu) + が (identifies who performs the action)]

たい焼きを食べていた *taiyaki o tabete ita*—ate *taiyaki*; was/were eating *taiyaki* [たい焼き (*taiyaki*; a Japanese fish-shaped pancake filled with red bean paste) + を (indicates the direct object of action) + 食べていた (from 食べる (to eat); ~ていた is used to describe a continuous action happening in the past; how to form: Verb て-form + いた)]

ことで *koto de*—by doing this [to highlight a method or means]

海外でも *kaigai demo*—even abroad [海外 (abroad; overseas) + でも (even)]

有名になりました *yuumei ni narimashita*—became famous [有名 (famous) + に (expresses the result of change) + なりました (became; polite past form of なる (to become; to turn; to reach; to attain))]

アニメ 「かのん」 で、月宮あゆがたい焼きを食べていたことで、海外
でも有名になりました。

あにめ　の　しゅじんこう　が　おいしそう　に　たべて　いる
と、じぶん　も　たべて　みたく　なります　よ　ね。にほん　に
きたら、ぜひ　たべて　みて　ください。

GLOSSARY AND NOTES

アニメの主人公が *anime no shujinkou ga*—the main character in the anime [アニメ (anime; animation; animated cartoon) + の (of; in; modifier) + 主人公 (hero; heroine; main character; protagonist) + が (identifies who performs the action)]

おいしそうに食べている *oishisou ni tabete iru*—is/are eating it with relish [おいしそうに (with relish; tastily; に is added to おいしそう (delicious-looking) to turn it into an adverbial form) + 食べている (is/are eating; ている-form of 食べる (to eat) which is used to describe an ongoing action)]

と *to*—when; if

自分 *jibun*—oneself; myself; yourself; himself; herself; you; I; me

も *mo*—too; also; as well

食べてみたくなります *tabete mitaku narimasu*—(it) makes (you) want to try to eat [from 食べる (to eat); 食べてみたく (continuative form of 食べてみたい (want to try to eat; ~てみたい is used to express that you want to try to do something for the first time which would imply that you will see if you like it or not) which is used to connect to the next verb なります) + なります (ます/polite form of なる (make; get into; become))]

よね *yo ne*—isn't that right? [a sentence ender which is used when you are less sure about opinions, information or knowledge]

日本に来たら *nihon ni kitara*—when (you) come to Japan [日本 (Japan) + に (to; expresses the direction and destination) + 来たら (from 来る (to come); ~たら means "when ~; if; after"; how to form: Verb (た form) + ら)]

ぜひ *zehi*—certainly; without fail; please; definitely

食べてみてください *tabete mite kudasai*—try eating (it); please try to eat [from 食べる (to eat); ~てみてください is used to express a demand, suggestion to someone to do something for the first time; how to form: Verb て-form + みてください]

アニメの主人公がおいしそうに食べていると、自分も食べてみたく
なりますよね。日本に来たら、ぜひ食べてみてください。

JAPANESE STREET FOOD, PART 2

"TAIYAKI"

Normal Speed

Slow Speed

Now, let's read the story once more in natural Japanese.
Lastly, check the English translation to make sure you understand.

鯛という魚の形をしたお菓子で、中にあんこがたっぷり入っています。明治時代から食べられています。あんこのかわりに、クリーム、チョコレート、キャラメルなどが入っていることもあります。アニメ「かのん」で、月宮あゆがたい焼きを食べていたことで、海外でも有名になりました。アニメの主人公がおいしそうに食べていると、自分も食べてみたくなりますよね。日本に来たら、ぜひ食べてみてください。

ENGLISH: (try to save this for last)

Taiyaki is a pancake that is shaped like a fish called "*tai* (sea bream)" and filled full of *anko* (sweet red bean jam). It has been eaten since the Meiji era (1868 - 1912). Instead of *anko*, it is sometimes filled with cream, chocolate, caramel, etc. *Taiyaki* became famous even abroad when Tsukimiya Ayu ate it in the anime "Kanon". When the main character in an anime is eating it with relish, it makes you want to try it too, right? When you come to Japan, you should definitely try one.

KEY VOCABULARY

日本のストリートフード *nihon no sutori-to fu-do*
—street food in Japan; Japanese street food

「たい焼き」　「*taiyaki*」—"taiyaki" [a Japanese fish-shaped cake filled with red bean paste]

あんこがたっぷり入っています *anko ga tappuri haitte imasu*—is well-filled with *anko* (red bean jam)

クリーム *kuri-mu*—cream

チョコレート *chokore-to*—chocolate

キャラメル *kyarameru*—caramel (soft candy)

海外 *kaigai*—abroad; overseas

主人公 *shujinkou*—main character; protagonist

ぜひ *zehi*—certainly; without fail; please; definitely

JAPANESE READER

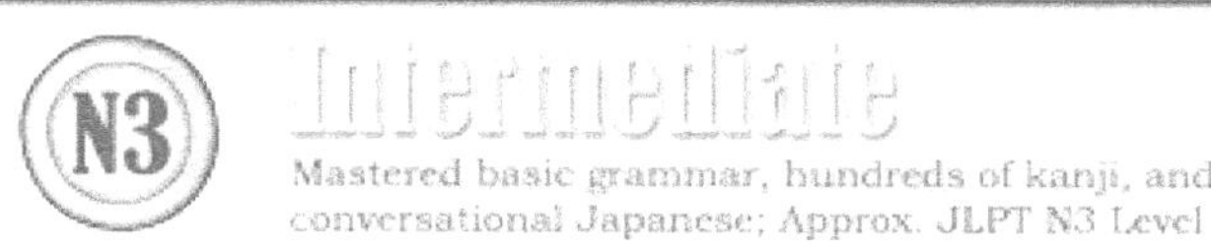

きっちょむさんと火事（かじ）

Kicchomu and the Fire

Story Read Normal

Story Read Slow Speed

Work through the story, sentence-by-sentence, referring to the vocabulary and grammar explanations below as needed.

むかしむかし、きっちょむさんという面白い人がいました。

きっちょむさんは、あわてもので よく失敗をしました。庄屋さ

んは、きっちょむさんに口うるさく、それを注意していまし

た。「きっちょむさん、お前はもっと落ち着かなくてはいけな

い。

きっちょむさん Kicchomu [a character often found in traditional stories from Oita prefecture]

と and (the fire)

火事 fire; conflagration [火 (fire); 事 (matter)]

むかしむかし long time ago

という such an (interesting person); named; called

面白い interesting; amusing (person)

人 person

がいました there existed

あわてもの scatterbrain; absent-minded person; careless; rash

で and [shows he was careless and therefore often made mistakes]

よく often (made mistakes)

失敗をしました made mistakes [失敗 (failure; mistake; blunder)]

庄屋さん village headman

に to (Kicchomu)

口うるさく nagging; faultfinding [literally, "mouth noisy"]

それを about that (Kicchomu's rash carelessness)

注意していました warned (him)

「」 (quotation markers)

きっちょむさん Mr. Kicchomu [even though the village headman is a little irritated with Kicchomu, he is still respectful and adds さん. Saying a name without an honorific is called 呼び捨て and can be considered to be very rude]

お前は as for you [お前 (you); は (topic marker)]

もっと more; -er

落ち着かなくてはいけない must calm down; (you) need to calm down [literally, "must not not be calm"]

どんなときもしっかり顔を洗って、きちんとした格好に着替え

て、それからよく考えてゆっくり行動しなさい。」

ある日、きっちょむさんが夜中に目が覚めると、庄屋さんの家

が火事になっていました。

どんなときも anytime; no matter the (situation); at all times [どんな (whatever; no matter what); とき (time); も (also; too; as well)]

しっかり carefully; firmly; properly; fully

顔を洗って wash (your) face and

きちんとした格好 neatly dressed; neat personal appearance [きちんとした (properly; precisely; neatly) modifies 格好 (shape; form; appearance)]

に着替えて change (clothes) into

それから and then

よく考えて think long and hard [よく (well); 考えて (think and)]

ゆっくり take (your) time; slowly; methodically

行動しなさい take action; (then) act

ある日 one day [the ある shows uncertainty: a certain day; one day]

が (marks the subject, sometimes the object)

夜中に in the middle of the night [夜中 (middle of the night; dead of night); に (in; at)]

目が覚める to wake up [literally, "eyes awaken"]

と and; upon (waking up)

庄屋さんの the headman's [庄屋さん (headman; village headman); の ('s)]

家 house

火事になっていました became a fire [火事 (fire; conflagration); に (expresses the result of change); なっていました (became)]

びっくりしたきっちょむさんは、あわてて庄屋さんに知らせに行こうと思いましたが、庄屋さんからいつもしつこく言われていることを思い出しました。「そうだ、まずは落ち着くことだ。それから、顔を洗って、着替えをして、そしてゆっくり歩いて知らせに行こう。」

びっくりしたきっちょむさん Kicchomu who was surprised; the surprised Kicchomu [びっくりした (surprised) modifies Kicchomu]

あわてて to be hurried; to hasten; to rush

庄屋さんに to the headman

知らせに in order to inform; to give the news [知らせ (news; tidings; information); に (in order to; for)]

行こう (intend) to go [volitional form of 行く (to go)]

と思いました thought [The と is a "quotation marker" that marks what he thought.]

が but

から from (the headman)

いつも always

しつこく insistently; persistently

言われている is being told; (constantly) told (that)

こと that; matter

思い出しました remembered

そうだ that's right; I see

まずは first of all

落ち着く to calm down; to compose oneself; to regain presence of mind

こと matter [nominalizes the previous verb]

だ is (copula)

それから and then

顔を洗って wash (my) face and

着替えをして change clothes and

そして and then

ゆっくり slowly; carefully

歩いて walk and

知らせに in order to inform; to tell

行こう (I'll) go

きっちょむさんは、お湯を沸かして、顔を洗い、髭も丁寧に剃

りました。それから一番いい着物に着替えて、ゆっくりと歩いて

庄屋さんの家に行きました。庄屋さんの家の戸の前で、とても静

かな声で礼儀正しく言いました。

お湯を沸かして boiled water and

顔を洗い washed face

髭も beard also; moustache also

丁寧に carefully; thoroughly

剃りました shaved

それから and then

一番いい the best [一番 (best; -est; #1); いい (good)]

着物 kimono; clothes

に着替えて changed into and

ゆっくりと slowly

歩いて walked and

庄屋さんの家 headman's house [庄屋さん (headman); の ('s); 家 (house)]

に行きました went to

庄屋さんの the headman's

家の戸 door of the house; house's door [家 (house); の

(of; 's; modifier); 戸 (door)]

の前 in front of; before (the door)

庄屋さんの家の戸の前 before the door of the head-man's house [when parsing long phrases with multiple の, it is often best to start at the end and work back. *before / the door / of the house / of the headman*]

で at (the door)

とても very

静かな quiet; soft (voice)

声で with (quiet) voice

礼儀正しく courteous; polite

言いました spoke; said

「庄屋さん、庄屋さん、ただ今、火事でございます。」ぼそぼそ

と小さな声で繰り返していると、庄屋さんがその声に気づいて起

きてきました。「なんじゃ？きっちょむ、どうした、こんな夜中

に？何しに来た？そんなにいい着物を着て？」

庄屋さん village headman

ただ今 just now [this is used to announce one's presence or to indicate something either just happened or is happening now]

火事 fire

でございます is; be [polite of です]

ぼそぼそと whispering; subdued; murmuring

小さな small; quiet

声 voice

で with (a quiet voice)

繰り返している was repeating

と and; upon doing so

その声 that voice

に気づいて realized and; noticed and

起きてきました woke up

なんじゃ？ what?; what's this?

どうした why; what's (wrong)

こんな such a (late night)

夜中に late in the night

何しに来た why did (you) come? [何 (what; why); し (to do; -masu form of する); に (for the purpose of); 来た (came)]

そんなに such a

いい着物 nice clothes [いい (nice; good; fine); 着物 (clothes; kimono; Japanese traditional clothing (especially full-length))]

いい着物を着て wearing (such) nice clothes

「はい、庄屋さん、こんばんは。お宅が火事でございます。」

「なに？」庄屋さんは、大慌てで火事を消し止めましたが、

きっちょむさんに向かってカンカンになって怒りました。

「きっちょむさん、こういう時は、夜中でもなんでも大きな声

をだして叫んで知らせてくれ。

はい yes [this is used to begin respectfully answering a question]

庄屋さん village headman

こんばんは good evening

お宅 (your) house

火事 fire

でございます is; are [polite of です]

なに？ what?

大慌てで with great haste; in a mad rush

火事を the fire (direct object)

消し止めました extinguished; put out [from 消し止める (to put out; to extinguish)]

が but; however

に向かって facing (Kicchomu)

カンカン furious; extremely angry; enraged

になって became (furious)

怒りました got angry; scolded

こういう時は in such a time as this [こういう (such as this); 時 (time; occasion); は (as for)]

夜中 middle of the night; late at night

でも even (in the middle of the night)

なんでも any; whatever; any kind of (loud voice)

大きな声をだして say with a loud voice [literally "put out a big voice"]

叫んで scream and; shout and

知らせてくれ tell me; inform me [くれ after the て form means "please do (something)" similar to ください]

きが
着替えなんかしなくてもいいから、早く来て、戸を破れんばか

はや き と やぶ
りにたたいてくれ。」「はい、かしこまりました。」

つぎ ひ よる
次の日の夜のことです。きっちょむさんは、大きな丸太を持っ

しょうや いえ い おお まるた も
て庄屋さんの家に行きました。そして、戸を破れんばかりに

まるた と やぶ
丸太でたたきました。

着替え change of clothes

なんか such as; things like; something like

しなくてもいい don't have to do

から therefore

早く来て hurry up and come and

戸 door

破れんばかりに as though (you are) about to bust

    down the door [破れん (to break); ばかりに as though about to (break the door); another way to put this would be 破れそうになるまで (until the point (the door) is about to break]

たたいて strike (the door) and; knock (on the door) and

くれ please do (verb) [when after the て form]

はい yes

かしこまりました I understand; certainly!

次の the next (day)

日 day

の夜 the night of

のこと happening (of the next night)

大きな big; large

丸太 log

を持って carrying (the log) and

庄屋さんの家 the village headman's house

に to (the house)

行きました went [past polite of 行く (to go)]

そして and then

戸を破れんばかりに until the door was about to break

    [破れん (to break); ばかりに as though about to (break the door); another way to put this would be 破れそうになるまで (until the point (the door) is about to break)]

丸太で with the log

たたきました knocked (on the door)

そして、大きな声で「火事だぁ！火事だぁ！」と叫び始めまし

た。「なに？また火事か？」と、庄屋さんが飛び出すと、火事な

どどこにも起こっていません。「きっちょむさん、もう叫ぶのは

やめてくれ。火事なんか起こってないじゃないか。」

そして and then

大きな声 loud voice [大きな (big; large; great; loud); 声 (voice)]

で with (a loud voice)

火事だぁ！ It's a fire!

と叫び始めました began to scream [と (quotation marker); 叫び (scream); 始めました (began to)]

なに？ what?

また again

火事 fire

か is it?

と (quotation marker)

庄屋さん village headman

飛び出す to jump out; to rush out [飛び (flying; leaping); 出す (to go out)]

と and; upon doing

火事 fire

など etc.; things like

どこにも nowhere [used with a negative verb]

起こっていません isn't happening

もう already; enough

叫ぶ to shout; to scream

のは regarding (the shouting)

やめてくれ please stop [やめて (stop); くれ (please do (verb); used after て verbs)]

火事 fire

なんか such a thing as; the likes of...

起こってない isn't occurring

じゃないか isn't it? don't you agree?

すると、きっちょむさんは、こう言いました。「はい、次に

火事が起こった時は、このくらいの起こし方でよろしいでしょ

うか？」

庄屋さんは、何も言えなかったそうです。

おしまい。

すると and then

こう言いました (Kicchomu) said

はい yes [used to politely show Kicchomu is answering the question]

次に the next; next time

火事が起こった there is a fire; (when) a fire occurs

時は when (there's a fire); the time of (a fire)

このくらいの about this level; about like this

起こし方 way of waking (you) [起こし (arousing; waking up); 方 (way of doing)]

で with (this way of waking)

よろしい is good; all right

でしょうか (question marker asking for confirmation)

何も nothing; not (able to say)

言えなかった not able to speak

そうです it seems; it appears that; I hear that...

おしまい the end

Kicchomu and the Fire

Please try to tackle the Japanese first and use this only as needed.

Once upon a time, there was an interesting man named Kicchomu. Kicchomu was a rash person who often made mistakes. The village headman used to nag him and warn him about it.

"Kicchomu, you need to calm down more. At all times, wash your face, dress properly, and then think carefully and act slowly."

One day, Kicchomu woke up in the middle of the night to find that the headman's house was on fire.

Surprised, he wanted to rush to the headman to inform him, but then he remembered what the headman was always telling him.

"Right. First I need to calm down. Then I'll wash my face, change my clothes, and then walk slowly to give him the news."

Kicchomu boiled water, washed his face, and carefully shaved. Then he changed into his best kimono and walked slowly to the headman's house.

He said politely in a very quiet voice in front of the door of the headman's house.

"Headman, headman, there is a fire at the present moment." As he repeated the words in a muffled voice, the headman woke up and noticed the voice.

"What is it? What's up, Kicchomu? What are you doing here so late? And wearing such a nice kimono?"

"Yes, Mr. Headman, good evening. Your house is on fire."

"What?"

The headman hurriedly put out the fire, but then became very angry with Kicchomu.

"Kicchomu, in times like this, even in the middle of the night, you should shout out loud and let me know. You don't need to change your clothes, just come quickly and bang on the door even if it breaks."

"Yes, sir."

The following night.

Kicchomu took a big log and went to the headman's house. He knocked on the door with the log so hard that it almost broke. Then, he said in a loud voice, "There's a fire! There's a fire! Fire!"

"What? Another fire?"

Continued

The headman jumped out but found that there was no fire anywhere.

"Kicchomu, please stop yelling. There's no fire."

Then he said, "Yes, sir, but the next time there's a fire, is this a good enough way to awaken you?"

The headman was speechless.

The end.

きっちょむさんと火事

　むかしむかし、きっちょむさんという面白い人がいました。きっちょむさんは、あわてものでよく失敗をしました。庄屋さんは、きっちょむさんに口うるさく、それを注意していました。「きっちょむさん、お前はもっと落ち着かなくてはいけない。どんなときもしっかり顔を洗って、きちんとした格好に着替えて、それからよく考えてゆっくり行動しなさい。」

　ある日、きっちょむさんが夜中に目が覚めると、庄屋さんの家が火事になっていました。

　びっくりしたきっちょむさんは、あわてて庄屋さんに知らせに行こうと思いましたが、庄屋さんからいつもしつこく言われていることを思い出しました。

　「そうだ、まずは落ち着くことだ。それから、顔を洗って、着替えをして、そしてゆっくり歩いて知らせに行こう。」

　きっちょむさんは、お湯を沸かして、顔を洗い、髭も丁寧に剃りました。それから一番いい着物に着替えて、ゆっくりと歩いて庄屋さんの家に行きました。

　庄屋さんの家の戸の前で、とても静かな声で礼儀正しく言いました。

　「庄屋さん、庄屋さん、ただ今、火事でございます。」
ぼそぼそと小さな声で繰り返していると、庄屋さんがその声に気づいて起きてきました。

　「なんじゃ？きっちょむ、どうした、こんな夜中に？何しに来た？そんなにいい着物を着て？」

　「はい、庄屋さん、こんばんは。お宅が火事でございます。」

Continued

「なに？」

　庄屋さんは、大慌てで火事を消し止めましたが、きっちょむさんに向かってカンカンになって怒りました。

　「きっちょむさん、こういう時は、夜中でもなんでも大きな声をだして叫んで知らせてくれ。着替えなんかしなくてもいいから、早く来て、戸を破れんばかりにたたいてくれ。」

　「はい、かしこまりました」

　次の日の夜のことです。

　きっちょむさんは、大きな丸太を持って庄屋さんの家に行きました。そして、戸を破れんばかりに丸太でたたきました。そして、大きな声で「火事だぁ！火事だぁ！」と叫び始めました。

　「なに？また火事か？」と、庄屋さんが飛び出すと、火事などどこにも起こっていません。

　「きっちょむさん、もう叫ぶのはやめてくれ。火事なんか起こってないじゃないか。」

　すると、きっちょむさんは、こう言いました。

　「はい、次に火事が起こった時は、このくらいの起こし方でよろしいでしょうか？」

　庄屋さんは、何も言えなかったそうです。

　おしまい。

Kanji in Focus

It is usually helpful to create a story based on the meanings of the kanji parts. Often, different kanji learning systems will use different "meanings" for the parts. We try to give the most common ones, but consistency is best. Choose one meaning per kanji part and stick with it. The following are a selection of the kanji found in this story. The <u>underlined</u> reading is probably the most used.

敗	READINGS / MEANING / EXAMPLE	<u>ハイ</u>・やぶれる failure; defeat; reversal しっぱい 失敗 failure; mistake; blunder	貝 shellfish; seashell; shell 攵 strike; hit In order to get this bucket of **seashells** 貝, you have to *defeat* them with just a **strike** 攵 on the ball.
意	READINGS / MEANING / EXAMPLE	<u>イ</u> idea; mind; heart; taste; thought; desire; care ちゅうい 注意 attention; notice; heed; caution; care	立 stand; rise; set up; erect 日 day; sun 心 heart; mind; spirit It's a good *idea* to **stand** 立 under the **sun** 日 to have a healthy body and **mind** 心.
着	READINGS / MEANING / EXAMPLE	<u>チャク</u>・ジャク・<u>きる</u>・~ぎ・きせる・~きせ・つく・つける arrive; wear き が 着替える to change (one's clothes)	羊 sheep ノ slanted line 目 eye; eyeball The kids *wear* a **sheep** 羊 costume with a design of **slanted line** ノ in the middle of an **eye** 目.
事	READINGS / MEANING / EXAMPLE	<u>ジ</u>・ズ・<u>こと</u>・つかう・つかえる matter; thing; fact; business; reason か じ 火事 fire; conflagration	一 one 口 mouth 彐 broom; hands 亅 feathered stick; barb **One** 一 *thing* to remember is that you must cover your **mouth** 口 with your **hands** 彐 while throwing away a rusty **barb** 亅 wire.
儀	READINGS / MEANING / EXAMPLE	<u>ギ</u> ceremony; rule; affair; case; a matter れい ぎ 礼儀 manners; courtesy; etiquette	亻 person; man; human 羊 sheep 手 hand; arm 戈 halberd; arms; weapon; spear It's part of the *ceremony* for a **man** 亻 to carry a **sheep** 羊 in his **arm** 手 before taking the **halberd** 戈.

Kanji in Focus Continued

屋	**READINGS** **MEANING** **EXAMPLE**	オク・や roof; house; shop; dealer; seller しょうや 庄屋 village headman (especially in the Kansai region)	尸 flag 一 one ム private; elbow 土 earth; dirt That house with a **flag** 尸 on the *roof* is **one** 一 of the **private** ム properties of the richest man on **earth** 土.
繰	**READINGS** **MEANING** **EXAMPLE**	ソウ・くる winding; reel; spin; turn (pages); look up; refer to く　かえ 繰り返す to repeat; to do something over again	糸 thread; yarn; string 品 goods; article; item; stock 木 tree; wood Pack this motor *winding* **thread** 糸 together with the handmade **goods** 品 made of **wood** 木.
怒	**READINGS** **MEANING** **EXAMPLE**	ド・ヌ・いかる・おこる angry; be offended おこ 怒る to get angry; to get mad	女 woman; female 又 again; once more; once again 心 mind; heart; spirit He is *angry* at that **woman** 女 **again** 又 and he keeps that feeling in his **heart** 心.
夜	**READINGS** **MEANING** **EXAMPLE**	ヤ・よ・よる night; evening にちや 日夜 day and night; around the clock; always	亠 lid 亻 person; man; human 夕 evening 乀 stretch She thinks that the one who forgot to put back the food container **lid** 亠 last *night*, is the **man** 亻 who came late that **evening** 夕 and had a **stretch** 乀 before eating.
起	**READINGS** **MEANING** **EXAMPLE**	キ・おきる・おこる・おこす・たつ rouse; wake up; get up お 起こす to raise up; to wake up; to waken	走 run 巳 stop, halt, previously, already, long ago *Get up* early to **run** 走 the race and don't **stop** 巳 till you reach the finish line.

Do you have any questions? Anything confusing? Feel free to email me (Clay) at clay@thejapanshop.com with any questions, comments, or suggestions.

Do you have ideas to make *Makoto* better? We'd love to hear from you. Did something particularly help you? Love to hear that as well.

What to experience even more Makoto? Learn about our new Makoto+ membership. Download the latest issue or access web-based back issues. All this and more starting at only $3. Go to: **www.MakotoPlus.com** now!

Clay & Yumi